Looking at Countries

GERMANY

Kathleen Pohl

FRANKLIN WATTS

LONDON·SYDNEY

This edition first published in 2008 by Franklin Watts

Franklin Watts
338 Euston Road
London NW1 3BH

Franklin Watts Australia
Level 17/207 Kent Street
Sydney, NSW 2000

First published in 2008 by Gareth Stevens Publishing
1 Reader's Digest Road
Pleasantville
NY 10570-7000 USA

Copyright © Gareth Stevens, Inc. 2008
Series design and concept, and text on pages 30–31 copyright © Franklin Watts 2008

Dewey number: 914.3
ISBN: 978 0 7496 8243 9

Senior Managing Editor: Lisa M. Guidone
Senior Editor: Barbara Bakowski
Creative Director: Lisa Donovan
Designer: Tammy West
Photo Researcher: Sylvia Ohlrich
Reading consultant: Susan Nations, M.Ed.

Photo credits: (t=top, b=bottom, l=left, r=right)
Cover (main) Greg Gawlowski/Lonely Planet Images; cover (inset) Torsten Krueger/Das Fotoarchiv/Peter
Arnold; title page Arco Images/Alamy; p. 4 Shutterstock; p. 6 Fridmar Damm/Zefa/Corbis; p 7t Masterfile; p. 7b
Klaus Hackenberg/Zefa/Corbis; p. 8 Harmut Schwarzbach/Argus/Peter Arnold; p. 9 Stefan Schuetz/Zefa/Corbis;
p. 10 Thomas Haertrich/Transit/Peter Arnold; p. 11t Damir Frkovic/Masterfile; p. 11b Wolfgang Rattay/Reuters
/Landov; p. 12 Imagebroker/Alamy; p. 13 vario images/Alamy; p. 14. Imagebroker/Alamy; p. 15t SuperStock; p.
15b W. Dieterich/Arco Images/Peter Arnold; p. 16 Peter Frischmuth/Argus/Peter Arnold;
p. 17t Robert Harding Picture Library Ltd./Alamy; p. 17b Peter Frischmuth/Argus/Peter Arnold;
p. 18 Markus Dlouhy/Das Fotoarchiv/Peter Arnold; p. 19t J. De Meester/Arco Images/Peter Arnold;
p. 19b F. Scholz/Arco Images/Peter Arnold; p. 20 Nigel Dickinson/Peter Arnold; p. 21t Franz-Marc Frei/
Corbis; p. 21b Torsten Krueger/Das Fotoarchiv/Peter Arnold; p. 22r Markus Dlouhy/Das Fotoarchiv/
Peter Arnold; p. 22l Helga Lade/Peter Arnold; p. 23t Ullstein-Schicke/Peter Arnold; p. 23b Manfred
Vollmer/Peter Arnold; p. 24 Sigrid Dauth/Alamy; p. 25l Robert Harding/Getty Images; p. 25r Stefan
Schuetz/Zefa/Corbis; p. 26 R. Kiedrowski/ArcoImages/Peter Arnold; p. 27t ImageState/Alamy;
p. 27b ImageState/Alamy. Every attempt has been made to clear copyright. Should there be any inadvertent
omission please apply to the publisher for rectification.

Printed in China

Franklin Watts is a division of Hachette Children's Books, an Hachette Livre UK company.
www.hachettelivre.co.uk

Contents

Where is Germany?

Germany is a large country in Central Europe. It shares borders with nine other countries. To the north is Denmark and to the east lie Poland and the Czech Republic. On the west, Germany borders the Netherlands, Belgium, Luxembourg and France. In the south are Switzerland and Austria.

Did you know?

The River Danube flows through southern Germany. It is Europe's second-longest river.

GERMANY

Atlantic Ocean

EUROPE

AFRICA

Indian Ocean

Germany has the largest population in the European Union.

Germany's lawmakers meet in this building in Berlin, its capital.

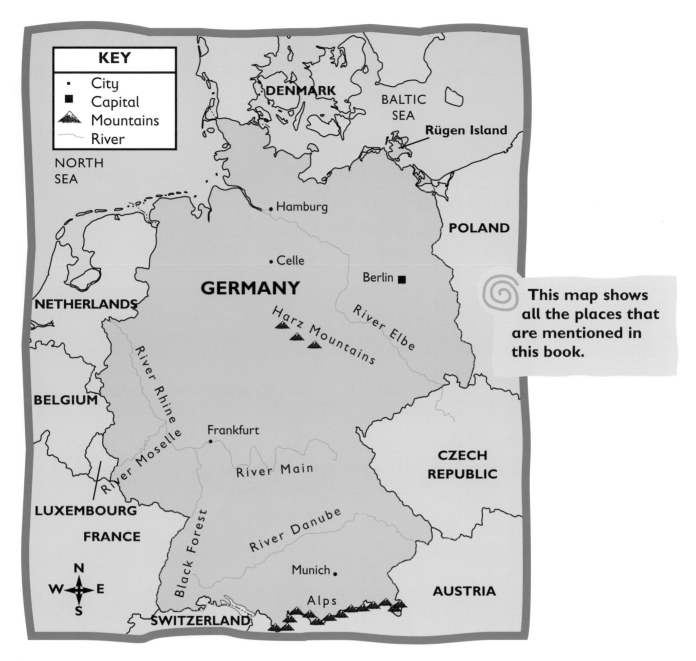

This map shows all the places that are mentioned in this book.

Germany has coastlines on the North Sea and the Baltic Sea. Some of the tiny islands in these seas are also part of Germany.

Berlin is the capital of Germany and its largest city. It is the centre of national government and the arts. Berlin has old churches and palaces, pretty parks and modern buildings.

The landscape

Northern Germany has many rivers and lakes. Sandy beaches line Germany's coasts along the North Sea and the Baltic Sea.

The white chalk cliffs of Rügen Island rise from the Baltic Sea.

Central Germany has hills, valleys and mountains. Many rivers flow through central and western Germany. They include the Rhine, the Moselle and the Main. The River Rhine is one of the world's busiest waterways.

Farms, villages and old castles line the banks of the River Rhine.

Tourists from all around the world visit southern Germany. They take walking holidays in the Black Forest and skiing trips in the Alps. The Alps are Germany's highest mountains. Zugspitz is the tallest peak, at 2,964 metres.

Did you know?

The Black Forest is the setting for many old German fairy tales.

The Black Forest got its name from the dark fir and spruce trees that grow there.

Weather and seasons

Germany's weather is mild and big changes in temperature are rare. Areas in the north-west and along the coast have warm summers. The winters there are mild and cloudy. Inland, the summers are warmer and the winters are a bit colder. The Rhine Valley, in western Germany, usually has the warmest summers.

Did you know?

In late autumn and early winter, south-eastern Germany sometimes has unusually warm weather. A warm wind called the *Foehn* (fern) can cause a big rise in temperature in just a few hours.

On warm days, Germans enjoy visiting this sandy beach on the Baltic Sea.

In the winter, tourists and local people enjoy walking, skiing and tobogganing in the snowy mountains of the German Alps.

Rainfall is moderate in most parts of Germany. July is both the hottest and rainiest month of the year as summer thunderstorms are common.

January is the coldest month. Snow falls mostly in the Alps, in southern Germany. Most other parts of Germany do not have much snowfall or freezing temperatures.

German people

For hundreds of years, Germany has produced great artists, composers and writers. Some of the world's best-loved music and children's stories come from Germany. *Grimm's Fairy Tales* are folk stories collected by the brothers Jakob and Wilhelm Grimm in the early 1800s. The most famous tales include 'Hansel and Gretel', 'Little Red Riding Hood' and 'Snow White'.

Germans enjoy folk dancing and special foods at festivals that celebrate their country's traditions.

Girls in traditional costumes dance at a folk festival.

Did you know?

German is the official language of Germany. Many people also speak English.

Religion is important to many people in Germany. More than one-third of Germans belong to Protestant churches, mostly Lutheran. Another third are Roman Catholic. Others are Muslim or Jewish.

On 3rd October, Germans celebrate Unity Day. It reminds people that Germany was once divided into two countries – East and West Germany – which became one nation again in 1990.

People visit the old Berlin Wall. It used to divide the city in two.

Germans celebrate Unity Day at the Brandenburg Gate in Berlin.

School

All children in Germany must go to school for at least nine years. They begin primary school at the age of six.

Students then move on to one of three kinds of secondary school around the age of 10 or 11. One type prepares students to train for jobs, another prepares them for business school. Students who pass a selective test go to a gymnasium school, for nine years and then usually on to university.

Almost all German schools are state schools and have no school fees.

Football is a favourite activity.

In most schools, the day begins at about 8 am and ends at about 1 pm. Many students come home from school to eat lunch with their families. Later in the afternoon, some children attend music school while others improve their sporting skills at clubs or classes.

The summer holiday lasts six weeks. Students also have shorter holidays during the year.

Did you know?

A teacher in Germany started the first school that was called a 'kindergarten'. The name comes from two German words that mean 'garden of children'.

Country

About 15 out of every 100 people in Germany live in the countryside. Most farms are small and family-owned. Farmers raise beef and dairy cattle, pigs and chickens. Wheat, barley, oats, sugar beet, potatoes and fruit are important crops.

Some farmers grow hops, a plant used to make beer. Along the Rhine and Moselle rivers, people grow grapes to make wine that is sold around the world.

A farmer harvests hops in a field.

These logs will be cut into planks at a sawmill.

Germany buys many food products from other countries. Farmers in Germany produce about two-thirds of the food eaten there.

Fishing boats float in the harbour of this coastal town.

Germany has many forests. Timber from the forests is used to build homes and make furniture. Wood is also used to make paper.

In fishing villages along Germany's coasts, people fish for herring and cod. About half of the fish comes from the North Sea.

City

Most people in Germany live in or near cities. Many cities have modern airports, offices and factories. The same cities may also have some very old buildings. More than three million people live in and around the capital, Berlin. It has many government buildings, playgrounds, zoos, theatres and more than 170 museums!

Did you know?

There is no speed limit on some German motorways.

People in Germany can travel quickly from city to city by train. High-speed motorways, called *autobahns*, connect all parts of the country.

Frankfurt is an important business centre with a modern skyline.

The Oktoberfest is a 16-day beer festival held each autumn in Munich.

Munich, Frankfurt and Hamburg are other big cities. Each is home to more than a million people. Hamburg, on the River Elbe, is Germany's biggest port. It is a centre of world trade. Munich is a major tourist city. Millions of people celebrate Oktoberfest there each autumn.

German homes

More than half of the people in Germany rent houses or flats instead of owning them. Some people live in old brick houses, others live in tall, modern blocks of flats. Town houses stand side by side in crowded cities.

Did you know?

People in Germany are building eco-homes that use very little energy for heating. Low-energy homes help save the planet from global warming.

In the city, most people live in terraced houses or blocks of flats.

Many houses are made of timber grown in Germany's forests. Half-timbered houses have wooden beams and brick or plaster on the outside walls. People fill their window boxes with colourful flowers.

This house is made of wood and has window boxes for flowers.

Half-timbered houses line the streets of Celle, in northern Germany.

Food

Germans enjoy many of the same foods as their European neighbours. They also eat German dishes, such as homemade noodles and sausages. *Sauerkraut*, pickled cabbage, is a popular food. Other favourites include potato dumplings and potato pancakes.

Did you know?

Many people in Germany enjoy an afternoon snack. It is called *Kaffee und Kuchen*, which means 'coffee and cakes'.

Germans love to eat spicy sausages. This shop has plenty to choose from!

Sauerkraut and *bratwurst* make a tasty meal. *Bratwurst* is a kind of German sausage.

People in Germany enjoy eating out at restaurants and pavement cafés.

Breakfast in Germany might include boiled eggs, bread or rolls with jam, cheese and cold meats. Lunch is the main hot meal of the day. Most people eat lunch at home. Many shops and offices close during the lunch hour. In the evening, Germans may eat a light supper at home or at a café.

At work

More than half of all Germans work as teachers, doctors, cooks, tour guides, office workers, shop assistants and bank clerks.

Manufacturing is a very important business. Workers make products such as cameras, electronics, tools and clothing. They also build ships and aeroplanes.

This man is blowing glass in a factory. Cities along eastern Germany's 'Glass Route' are known for their fine glassware.

German-made cuckoo clocks are sold around the world.

Germans take great pride in the cars they make.

A steel mill is a hot place to work!

Germany's natural resources include iron ore, which is used to make steel. Mills in the cities make much of the steel for German car-makers. Germany is the world's third-largest producers of cars. Only Japan and the United States of America build more cars.

Having fun

People in Germany like to have fun in their free time. Most workers get about two months holiday a year. Many people spend some of that time enjoying their beautiful country. They walk and cycle in the Black Forest or sail on the River Rhine. Some people visit old castles. Many Germans travel with their families to other countries, too.

Did you know?

Beethoven, Bach and Brahms are three famous German composers. Although they lived over 200 years ago, their music is still popular today.

People like to walk, cycle and ski on trails in the Black Forest.

Tourists love to visit this castle in the Alps. It is known as Mad King Ludwig's castle.

Winter sports in the Alps are fun for the whole family!

People of all ages like going to clubs where they play many different sports. Football is the most popular sport in Germany. Some people enjoy mountain climbing in the Alps and ice-skating.

People in Germany like to watch television and go to the cinema. They also listen to music and go to the opera.

Germany: the facts

- Germany is a federal republic. The country's official name is the Federal Republic of Germany.

- The president is the head of state. The chancellor handles the daily tasks of running the government.

- Germany is a member of the European Union.

- About 82 million people live in Germany. It has the biggest population of any country in the European Union. In recent years, many people from other countries have come to live in Germany.

This castle in Dortmund, north-west Germany, is about 800 years old. A deep moat helped to keep the castle safe from enemies.

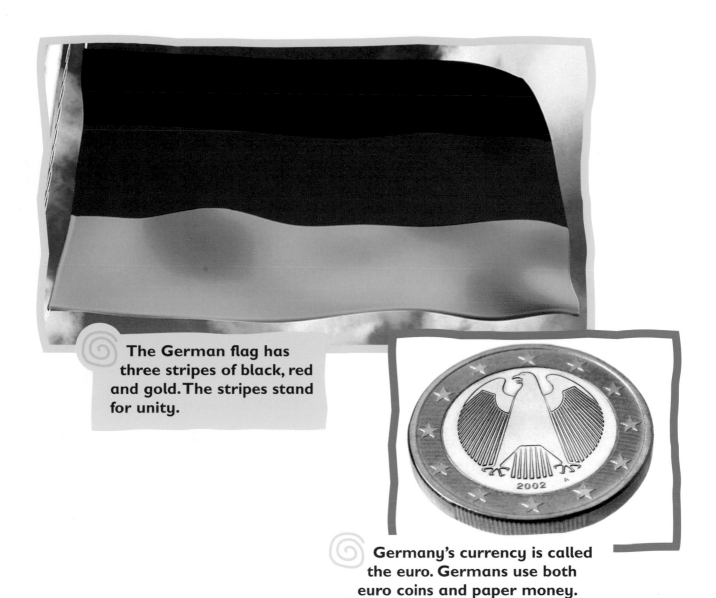

The German flag has three stripes of black, red and gold. The stripes stand for unity.

Germany's currency is called the euro. Germans use both euro coins and paper money.

Did you know?

Russia is the only European country that has a bigger population than Germany. (Russia is not in the European Union.)

Germany and many other member countries of the European Union use the same currency, or money. It is called the euro. Euro paper money looks the same in all those nations. The fronts of euro coins also look the same. The backs of the coins vary from country to country.

Glossary

Autobahns high-speed cross-country roads or motorways.

Chancellor in some European countries, a leader who handles the daily tasks of running the government.

Composers people who write music.

Euro the currency, or money, used by most of the member countries of the European Union.

European Union a group of countries in Europe that work together in trade and politics.

Federal republic a system in which the national government and the states have separate powers, with elected officials representing the people.

Foehn a warm, dry wind that blows down the slopes of the Alps in south-eastern Germany.

Global warming a rise in the temperature of the Earth that may be due to the increase of certain gases in the atmosphere.

Gymnasium a secondary school that prepares students for university.

Head of state the main representative of a country.

Hops the small, green, cone-shaped flowers of the hop plant, used in making beer.

Manufacturing the making of goods by hand or machine.

Natural resources things supplied by nature, such as forests and minerals, that are used by people.

Oktoberfest a beer festival held each year in Munich.

Opera a play set to music.

Rent to pay money to the owner for the use of a house or a flat.

Sauerkraut cabbage that has been cut up and salted, and allowed to become sour.

Tourists people who travel to places for fun.

Find out more

www.ukgermanconnection.org/kids_new/?location_id=4
Join the Voyage Kids and explore many areas of German life, culture and language.

http://news.bbc.co.uk/cbbcnews/hi/guides/default.stm
For more information about how the European Union works, click on 'European Union' in the list of Newsround guides.

Note to parents and teachers: Every effort has been made by the Publishers to ensure that these websites are suitable for children, that they are of the highest educational value, and that they contain no inappropriate or offensive material. However, because of the nature of the Internet, it is impossible to guarantee that the contents of these sites will not be altered. We strongly advise that Internet access is supervised by a responsible adult.

Some German words

German word	English word	Say ...
guten Tag	hello	gooten tahk
auf Wiedersehen	goodbye	owf veeder-zayn
ja	yes	ya
nein	no	nine
bitte	please	bi-te
angenehm	pleased to meet you	an-genaym
danke	thank you	dang-ke
Wie geht's?	How are you?	vee gayts
Danke, gut	Fine, thanks	dang-ke goot
Wie bitte?	Pardon?	vee bi-te
Ich verstehe nicht	I don't understand	ikh fer-shtay-e nikht
Bis morgen	See you tomorrow	bis morgen

My map of Germany

Trace this map, colour it in and use the map on page 5 to write the names of all the towns.

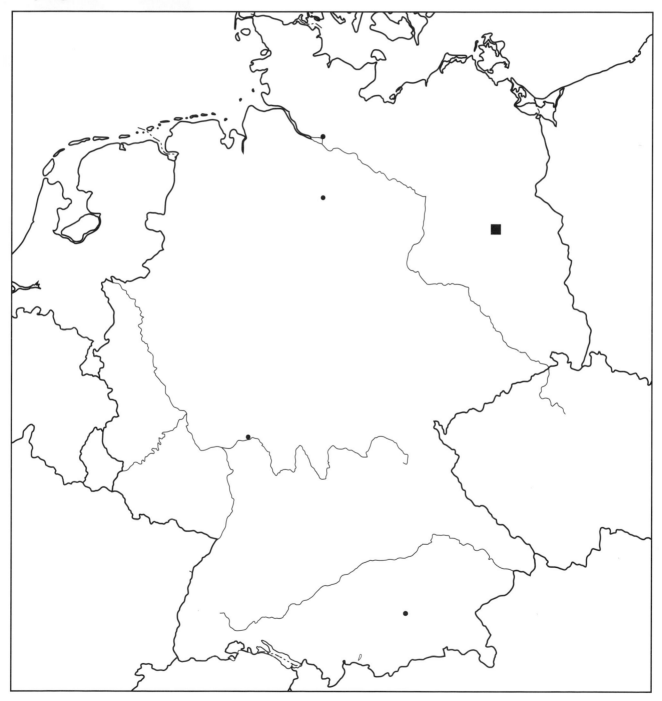

Index